W9-BBS-897

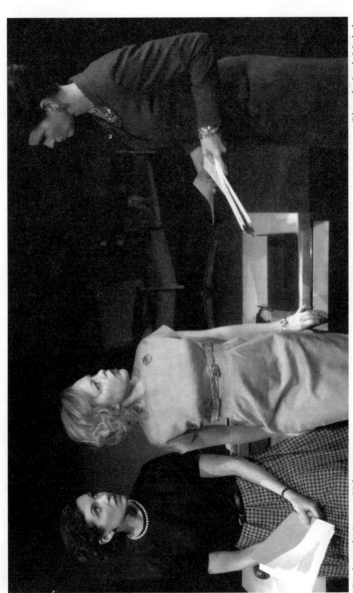

Set design by Lauren Helpern

Photo by Leah Michalos

Sarah Wilson, Alicia Sable and Amy Wilson in a scene from the HERE production of *The Best of Everything*.

# THE BEST OF EVERYTHING

ADAPTED BY
## JULIE KRAMER

BASED ON THE BOOK BY
## RONA JAFFE

★

★

DRAMATISTS
PLAY SERVICE
INC.

**SPECIAL NOTE**

Anyone receiving permission to produce THE BEST OF EVERYTHING is required to give credit to the Author as sole and exclusive Author of the Play on the title page of all programs distributed in connection with performances of the Play and in all instances in which the title of the Play appears for purposes of advertising, publicizing or otherwise exploiting the Play and/or a production thereof. The name of the Author must appear on a separate line, in which no other name appears, immediately beneath the title and in size of type equal to 50% of the size of the largest, most prominent letter used for the title of the Play. No person, firm or entity may receive credit larger or more prominent than that accorded the Author. The billing must appear as follows:

THE BEST OF EVERYTHING
adapted by Julie Kramer
based on the book by Rona Jaffe

In addition, the following acknowledgment must appear on the title page in all programs distributed in connection with performances of the Play:

Developed with Amy Wilson

**SPECIAL NOTE ON SONGS AND RECORDINGS**

For performances of copyrighted songs, arrangements or recordings mentioned in this Play, the permission of the copyright owner(s) must be obtained. Other songs, arrangements or recordings may be substituted provided permission from the copyright owner(s) of such songs, arrangements or recordings is obtained; or songs, arrangements or recordings in the public domain may be substituted.

*For my parents Rita and Howard Kramer,*
*my husband Niko Triantafillou,*
*and Amy Wilson, my friend.*

# ACKNOWLEDGMENTS

So many people helped to make this play possible: Robert Wishnew, Richard Agins, and The Rona Jaffe Foundation; Jenny Lyn Bader, David Diamond, Bixby Elliot, Benjamin Feldman, David Flannery, Nagle Jackson, Jill Kurland-Rak, Leah Michalos, Jessica Provenz, Robin Rothstein; Beth Blickers and Peter Hagan and everyone at Abrams; the wonderful actors from the readings at The Directors Company and New Georges; my spectacular cast from the HERE production; my darling casting director Paul Davis; my designers who helped me better understand my own work through their brilliant artistry; my beautiful stage manager Katharine Whitney who kept me almost sane; Susan Bernfield who gives me endless advice in all things, and whose support sustains my artistic life; and Wendy Weiner, who read this script more times than I can count and always believed in it and in me. And because it bears repeating, Amy Wilson, for Everything.

THE BEST OF EVERYTHING was presented by 95 WordsPer-Minute and Hyde Park & Lafayette LLC at HERE in New York City, opening on Sept 29, 2012. It was directed by Julie Kramer; the set design was by Lauren Helpern; the lighting design was by Graham Kindred; the costume design was by Daniel Urlie; the sound design was by Jill BC DuBoff; the production stage manager was Katharine Whitney; the associate producer was Holly Rosen Fink; the general manager was Leah Michalos; and the casting was by Paul Davis/Calleri Casting. The cast was as follows:

CAROLINE ............................................................ Sarah Wilson
BRENDA ............................................................... Sas Goldberg
MARY AGNES ....................................................... Molly Lloyd
APRIL .................................................................... Alicia Sable
MISS FARROW ...................................................... Amy Wilson
GREGG .................................................................. Hayley Treider
EDDIE ................................................................... Jordan Geiger
MIKE RICE/MR. SHALIMAR/
DAVID WILDER SAVAGE/RONNIE .................. Tom O'Keefe
VOICEOVER ......................................................... Susan Bott

THE BEST OF EVERYTHING also had a workshop in April 2011 as part of "This is Your Week" at New Georges: Susan Bernfield, Producing Artistic Director; Sarah Cameron Sunde, Deputy Artistic Director; Jaynie Saunders Tiller, Managing Director; Kara-Lynn Vaeni, Literary Manager.

THE BEST OF EVERYTHING had an invited reading in June 2010 at The Directors Company, Michael Parva, Artistic Director; Leah Michalos, Managing Director.

# AUTHOR'S NOTE

This play works best when performed with a nod to 1940s and '50s performance style — a slightly heightened manner, quick cue pick-up. But it should never be campy. These girls mean what they say, completely and utterly. For them the stakes are very real.

While a lot has changed for women since the '50s, a surprising amount hasn't. So as a director I embraced contemporary theatrical devices such as the toy-sized ship and the Men in the Grey Flannel Suit cardboard cutouts. The ship should be both kind of silly and rather lovely. In the New York production it was small enough to be easily held in two hands, but it still conveyed a sense of physical and emotional import. The cardboard cutout men should be handsome but generic.

This is a story about the girls in the typing pool, not the men in the offices, so most of the male characters are played by one actor. Only Eddie is played by a separate actor, because to Caroline, he's not like all the others. Whether she's right about that or not remains to be seen.

# CHARACTERS

CAROLINE BENDER (Early 20s.) Pretty and very smart with a broken heart beneath her polished exterior.

BRENDA ZALESKI (20s.) A schemer with slight Queens accent.

MARY AGNES RUSSO (20s.) Naïve and gossipy but in a funny rather than mean-spirited way.

APRIL MORRISON (Early 20s.) Beautiful small-town girl. Says funny things without knowing they're funny. Catnip to men (and doesn't really know that either).

AMANDA FARROW (Mid-to-late 30s.) Smart, put-together and intimidating. Unmarried at 36, she's the only female editor at Fabian Publishing, and determined to keep it that way.

GREGG ADAMS (Early 20s.) An actress and a temp. She has the face of a 16-year-old and the sophistication of a 40-year-old. Not as devil-may-care as she seems.

EDDIE HARRIS (Early 20s.) Caroline's ex-fiancé. Harvard man. Sees himself as the hero of a romantic novel.

*One actor plays the following roles:*

MIKE RICE (40s.) Handsome but dissipated. An alcoholic and a cynic but a good man.

DAVID WILDER SAVAGE (30s.) Dashing, smart, the devil. Makes every woman feel like the only girl in the world.

MR. SHALIMAR (60s.) The editor-in-chief of Fabian Publishing. Sophisticated, with a possibly affected British accent and lots of impressive stories. A drinker and garter snapper of the worst order.

RONNIE WOOD (20s.) Small-town boy, handsome, sweet, a slight stutter.

## PLACE

Desks, chairs and props become the typing pool
and offices of Fabian Publishing.

## TIME

September 1952 – January 1954.

# THE BEST OF EVERYTHING

### Scene 1

*In darkness, the sound of a ship's horn. Lights come up on a toy-sized cruise ship.*

*Caroline Bender enters. She's waving her handkerchief and looking longingly at the ship.*

*Eddie Harris enters. While he and Caroline are not literally together, it's nice if there can be some sense of connection between them during the following.*

EDDIE.  Dear Caroline, This is the fourth letter I've written to you, the other three efforts I've torn up. These six weeks in Europe have changed me so. How much easier it is to declare love than to withdraw it, especially from someone you still like very much. *(Caroline stops waving.)* By now you know I'm not on the ship. *(Caroline walks to the ship and looks at it closely.)* Instead, I will be returning with Helen Lowe and her parents to Dallas, and marrying Helen next month. *(Caroline picks up the ship and stares at it, as if it were Eddie's letter.)* I hope you appreciate how unpleasant a predicament this is for me. You are lucky you have only to read this letter rather than write it. I certainly wish you the best of everything. Eddie. *(Lights shift. Music, upbeat but jarring. Caroline stands in shock as Mary Agnes, April and Gregg rush in and start setting up the typing pool. One of them takes the ship out of Caroline's hands and puts it in a filing cabinet. Brenda enters and makes a beeline for Caroline as the music fades. Brenda is from Queens.)*

BRENDA. How do you want your coffee? You'd better take it in a jar instead of a paper container.

CAROLINE. *(Thrown.)* Coffee? Thank you. *(Brenda exits, and Mary Agnes rushes over. Mary Agnes has a lot to say.)*

MARY AGNES. That's Brenda. Watch out for her. She makes you pay for the coffee and the jar, and then she gives back the jars and keeps all the deposit money. Don't let her get away with it.

CAROLINE. Okay.

MARY AGNES. Did you notice her teeth? She's engaged to be married and she's having all her bad teeth pulled so her husband will have to pay for the new ones. Did you ever hear of such a thing?

CAROLINE. I don't think that I have. I'm Caroline Bender.

MARY AGNES. I'm Mary Agnes Russo. You can have that desk. *(She points to the closest one.)*

CAROLINE. I'd like to get started. Is there anything for me to type?

MARY AGNES. Oh there's plenty of time for all that. Miss Farrow comes in around ten o'clock. She'll take you around and introduce you to everybody.

CAROLINE. Miss Farrow? Is she the head secretary?

MARY AGNES. Don't let her hear you say that! She's an editor!

CAROLINE. I didn't know women could be editors. I thought they could only be secretaries.

MARY AGNES. Well, Miss Farrow is the only female editor at Fabian Paperbacks. She wears her hat in the office all day long just so no one will mistake her for one of us. She's 36 and she's not married! *(Beat.)* You'll be working for her temporarily because her secretary quit.

CAROLINE. Me?

MARY AGNES. We have a temp, Gregg Adams, but she's not here every day because she's an actress. Do you have plans for lunch?

CAROLINE. No. Would you like to eat together?

MARY AGNES. Oh, I can't. I always have lunch with my boyfriend. Some days he brings his lunch up here, and some days I bring my sandwiches downtown. We're saving up to get married one year from this coming June. *(April Morrison rushes in. She has messy blonde hair and a beautiful face, and she's so small town she should be carrying a sunbonnet.)*

APRIL. Oh my goodness! Am I terribly late?

MARY AGNES. Yes.

APRIL. I was so excited for my very first job I forgot to set my alarm.

CAROLINE. It's my first job as well. I'm Caroline.

APRIL. I'm April Morrison from Springs Colorado. I just graduated from junior college. My parents gave me five hundred dollars and a bus ticket for my present and said I could stay as long as the money lasted. It's been two weeks and I just don't know where it all went! So I said to myself, "April Morrison, you belong here. Get yourself a job." And here I am! *(As April talks, Mike Rice walks across the typing pool. He seems mid-40s, and looks like he's had a rough night. He's wearing a camel's-hair coat with a large cigarette burn on the lapel. He looks at the girls, then heads to his office.)*

CAROLINE. Who's that?

MARY AGNES. Mike Rice. He's the editor of *The Cross.*

CAROLINE. The religious magazine? He doesn't seem like the type.

MARY AGNES. Have you read *The Cross*? It will sicken you.

CAROLINE. It's very pious.

APRIL My Nana loves *The Cross.*

MARY AGNES. He writes those articles, but he doesn't believe in anything. He hangs around in those Third Avenue bars every night, drinking and reciting poetry and talking to any stranger he can lay his hands on.

CAROLINE. He's not married?

MARY AGNES. He had a wife, but she left him. He lives in a real rundown hotel on the West Side. He has a daughter ten years old who he never sees.

APRIL. Oh how sad!

MARY AGNES. *(Kind.)* I always feel sorry for a person like him. If he was married and lived with his wife and child he wouldn't be like that.

CAROLINE. *(Upset.)* So marriage solves everything?

MARY AGNES. *(Explaining.)* There are only two ways to live, the right way and the wrong way. If you live the right way you're happy, and if you live the wrong way you're miserable. If you get married it doesn't mean positively you're going to be happy, but if you get married and walk out on it then you can't be happy. You'll always know you gave up on a responsibility.

CAROLINE. What if the other person walks out on you?

MARY AGNES. *(Eyes widening.)* Were *you* married?

CAROLINE. Engaged.

APRIL. Oh how terrible.

MARY AGNES. I'll never talk about it again. Unless you bring it up. If you ever want to talk about it, you just tell me.

CAROLINE. I took this job so I would have something else to talk about. *(Miss Farrow enters. She's slim and fashionable and wearing a chic hat. She looks at Caroline and April.)*

AMANDA. Which one is mine?

MARY AGNES. *(Jumping in.)* This is Caroline Bender, Miss Farrow.

CAROLINE. I'm so pleased to have the opportunity to — *(Miss Farrow starts walking to her office.)*

AMANDA. Come. *(Caroline follows.)* First you can order me some coffee from the coffee shop downstairs, black with sugar. All the filing to be done is in that box. My secretary left last week and the place is a mess. The mail comes four times a day, you open it, and anything that requires a personal answer goes in that box. *(She points.)* Some of the letters you can answer yourself, if they're from cranks, for instance. But show me everything you write before you send it out. Everything you do has to go through me first. You get one hour for lunch and I want you back here on time so you can answer my phone. Oh, and Miss Bender, if Mr. Bossart calls make sure you put him right through. He's the vice-president of the company. We have a very important relationship. *(Caroline is trying to take notes.)*

CAROLINE. I'm sorry Miss Farrow. Which box is for mail that requires a personal response? *(Amanda points.)* Thank you. And how will I know if something requires a personal response?

AMANDA. That is an excellent question, Miss Bender. I would say to use your common sense, but it is becoming apparent that you have none. So open everything and let me see it all.

CAROLINE. Of course, Miss Farrow. *(Caroline picks up the phone.)*

AMANDA. *(Aghast.)* What are you doing?

CAROLINE. Calling the coffee shop?

AMANDA. Not here! You use your phone outside. You always answer my line at the telephone on your desk and say "Miss Farrow's office." Do you think you can manage that?

CAROLINE. Yes, Miss Farrow.

AMANDA. Wonderful. *(Beat.)* The coffee? *(Caroline returns to her desk. Mary Agnes swoops in.)*

MARY AGNES. How do you like your new boss?

CAROLINE. So far it's like hell week for getting into a sorority.

MARY AGNES. Hey that's cute!

12

CAROLINE. I'm glad she's only my temporary boss. I was an excellent student, but Miss Farrow seems to think I'm a complete fool.

MARY AGNES. It's not personal. She treats all of us that way.

CAROLINE. I'd like to make a good impression.

MARY AGNES. I wouldn't count on it. She always says she wants a secretary like you, a college graduate who's pretty and sophisticated, and then she always hates the poor girl's guts. *(April enters.)*

APRIL. Caroline! I'm working for someone important also. Mr. Shalimar. He's the editor-in-chief!

MARY AGNES. His regular secretary is sick.

APRIL. He is the most fascinating person I have ever met. He knew Eugene O'Neill! *(Caroline's phone rings. She picks up.)*

CAROLINE. *(Tentative.)* Miss Farrow's office? Yes, Miss Farrow. I was just about to call the coffee shop. I'm sorry, Miss Farrow. *(She hangs up and puts her head in her hands, then takes a breath.)* Please excuse me, April, I have some work to do.

APRIL. Of course! It's so busy here. Mr. Shalimar said he may need me to work through lunch, and he'll pay for the sandwiches! I've been so *hungry* since I got to New York. I can't afford anything but Fig Newtons for supper! *(Caroline picks up the phone and dials as April exits.)*

CAROLINE. Hello operator, please connect me to the coffee shop downstairs. *(Listening.)* Good morning, I'd like to place an order for Miss Farrow. One coffee, black with sugar. Whose account? Hers, I suppose? Thank you. *(She hangs up. The phone rings and she answers.)* Miss Farrow's office. Mr. Bossart? One moment please. *(Caroline looks at the buttons on the phone, panicked. Mary Agnes comes over and presses a button.)* Mr. Bossart for you, Miss Farrow. *(She exhales, relieved, and turns to Mary Agnes.)* Thank you!

MARY AGNES. You're welcome. *(Beat.)* People say she's having an affair with him. Mr. Bossart.

CAROLINE. Really?

MARY AGNES. They say that's how she got to be the only female editor.

CAROLINE. Do you think that's true?

MARY AGNES. I don't. He's a married man!

CAROLINE. I thought that sort of thing only happened in Fabian Paperbacks. That is terrible, to … be with … someone else's husband.

MARY AGNES. I know.

CAROLINE. Maybe people say that out of jealousy. It must be difficult to become an editor without stepping on people's toes.

MARY AGNES. Some people have nothing better to do than gossip. *(Beat.)* Listen, if she asks if you want to be promoted and be her private secretary, say no! Even though they make sixty-five dollars a week.

CAROLINE. Sixty-five is a lot better than the fifty I'm getting now.

MARY AGNES. Being a private secretary is a lot of work. Most of the girls who do it want to get into editorial work and be a reader. That pays seventy-five dollars a week.

CAROLINE. *(Intrigued.)* You get to read manuscripts all day? That sounds like a wonderful job.

MARY AGNES. I hate to read. *(Caroline's phone rings. She answers.)*

CAROLINE. Yes, Miss Farrow. I'll be right in. *(She hangs up.)* I'd better go.

MARY AGNES. She'll go to lunch soon. She leaves around 11:30 and doesn't come back until three. Sometimes she doesn't come back at all!

CAROLINE. How does she get any work done?

MARY AGNES. Executives don't do the work. The higher up you get the less you have to do. Until you're the top man, and then you have to make the decisions, and that's hard. It's the ones just under the top who have the best deal. See you later, Caroline. *(As Caroline heads to Miss Farrow's office, Brenda enters.)*

BRENDA. Mary Agnes, wait until I tell you! Mr. Shalimar is "training" the new girl! Come quick! *(Caroline continues to Miss Farrow's office. Lights up on Miss Farrow, editing a manuscript.)*

CAROLINE. I ordered your coffee, Miss Farrow. I charged it to your account.

AMANDA. What's the matter, didn't you have any money?

CAROLINE. As a matter of fact, I didn't.

AMANDA. That's funny. I thought that you were another one of those Vassar girls who wants to be an editor just because she majored in English. *(Caroline doesn't respond.)* Well, Miss Bender?

CAROLINE. I … went to Radcliffe, Miss Farrow.

AMANDA. *(Unimpressed.)* Oh. Did you.

CAROLINE. I did major in English.

AMANDA. And now you think it's easy to be an editor.

CAROLINE. I'm not even sure it's easy to be a secretary.

AMANDA. It's not easy to be my secretary. *(Beat.)* Do you know that for this typing job you have we turned away fifteen other girls?

CAROLINE. That's what they told me at the employment agency.

AMANDA. What makes you think you have more of a right to be here than any of those fifteen girls? A degree in English from Radcliffe?

CAROLINE. I don't know those girls, Miss Farrow. But I've just finished six weeks of a business and secretarial course. I love books. And I'd like to learn from you.

AMANDA. Are you just here until you get married?

CAROLINE. I don't plan on getting married anytime soon.

AMANDA. Really. So you're one of the ambitious ones?

CAROLINE. *(Considers it.)* Ambitious? I don't think so.

AMANDA. Miss Bender, most young girls are like your new friend, Mary Agnes. Their only ambition is to do their work satisfactorily, disappear at five o'clock on the dot, and line up at the bank on payday. Then there are the eager newcomers, the fomenters, hoping to find a vice-president to throw the caste system aside after a few Scotches, so they can become his mistress and advance their career. I suggest you decide which kind of girl you want to be. Otherwise someone else will make that decision for you.

CAROLINE. Thank you, Miss Farrow. I will. *(Amanda looks at her almost appreciatively.)*

AMANDA. Get to work.

## Scene 2

*It's six P.M. Friday, the end of Caroline's first week. She's in the typing pool alone, typing and referring to the manuscript in front of her. Mike Rice comes out of his office.*

MIKE RICE. The enthusiasm of youth.

CAROLINE. Mr. Rice. Hello.

MIKE RICE. If old man Fabian had only known, he wouldn't have bothered to pay you kids for working here, he would have charged you.

CAROLINE.  I want to finish this before Mr. Shalimar leaves for the weekend.

MIKE RICE.  Mr. Shalimar is meeting me downstairs for a drink. He won't do any work before Monday. I'm certain you have better things to do on a Friday night than concern yourself with the fate of *(He leans over and looks at the manuscript.) Beautiful Bodies.*

CAROLINE.  It was either *Beautiful Bodies* or a blind date with Alvin Wiggs. He works in his father's mannequin business.

MIKE RICE.  A blind date?

CAROLINE.  An old American institution of mismating. You haven't been on one?

MIKE RICE.  I married when I was eighteen. Besides no one I knew cared whether I had a social life or not.

CAROLINE.  Well, everyone in Port Blair is very concerned with mine. But I prefer to read a good book. I thought *Beautiful Bodies* would be enjoyable — Miss Farrow wrote on her comment sheet that it was wonderful. It seemed exciting to be able to read something like that before it was even published.

MIKE RICE.  And was it exciting?

CAROLINE.  My job is to type what Miss Farrow thinks.

MIKE RICE.  You strike me as the curious sort.

CAROLINE.  To be frank? I thought it was downright dull. It's made me wonder if I'm in the wrong field entirely.

MIKE RICE.  People buy Fabian Paperbacks for the titles. Miss Farrow is smart. *Beautiful Bodies* not only sounds racy, it sounds like the title of someone else's successful book.

CAROLINE.  *(Passionate.)* But just imagine if the book were as good as the title. People would tell their friends how much they liked it and more people would buy it. And they would be more likely to keep buying Fabian Paperbacks if the books delivered what was promised.

MIKE RICE.  *(Leaning close.)* You know something? You're *damn* smart.

CAROLINE.  *(Flustered, but flattered.)* Thank you.

MIKE RICE.  Be careful who knows it.

CAROLINE.  And here I thought that was a compliment.

MIKE RICE.  You're a kid with brilliant instincts. That bugs some people. I happen to like it. *(He pats her cheek and tosses his camel's hair coat over one shoulder.)* Now if you'll excuse me, I have a date with a bar stool. Let Mr. Shalimar know I'm at The Unfriendly

Irishman. *(Mike exits. Caroline starts typing. Mr. Shalimar enters. Ideally the transition from Mike to Mr. Shalimar is acknowledged in some theatrical way. Mr. Shalimar has a possibly affected British manner of speaking.)*

CAROLINE. Mr. Shalimar?

MR. SHALIMAR. Yes.

CAROLINE. Mr. Rice said to let you know that he's downstairs at The Unfriendly Irishman.

MR. SHALIMAR. Thank you, young lady. *(Mr. Shalimar starts to leave, and Caroline calls out.)*

CAROLINE. I'm working on a report for you. On this manuscript, *Beautiful Bodies?*

MR. SHALIMAR. Ah yes, one of Miss Farrow's. Whatever she recommends is fine.

CAROLINE. Yes, sir. *(Mr. Shalimar starts to leave.)* Mr. Shalimar? I would be so interested to know what you think of it. Whether it's … up to Fabian's standards. *(He turns.)*

MR. SHALIMAR. I have extremely high standards for Fabian. Do you realize there are towns in America where there are no libraries or bookstores? The only place people can get a book is at the drugstore. And do you know what they read?

CAROLINE. Fabian Paperbacks?

MR. SHALIMAR. Exactly! We are responsible for the changing literary taste of America.

CAROLINE. How wonderful! *(Mr. Shalimar moves closer.)*

MR. SHALIMAR. You want experience.

CAROLINE. Yes.

MR. SHALIMAR. I'll give you experience. I've been forty years an editor. I've taught some of the best writers in the business. I knew Eugene O'Neill.

CAROLINE. Your guidance would be so valuable.

MR. SHALIMAR. What is your name, young lady?

CAROLINE. Caroline Bender.

MR. SHALIMAR. I'll tell you what. For the next week or two I'll give you a manuscript every night to take home and read. You give me a report on each one.

CAROLINE. So I'll be a reader?

MR. SHALIMAR. A reader? No. You'll be a very lucky secretary. *(Mr. Shalimar exits. Caroline finishes Miss Farrow's report and puts it on top of the manuscript. April comes out of Mr. Shalimar's office, smoothing wrinkles from her skirt, and sees Caroline.)*

APRIL. Oh, Caroline. Hello.

CAROLINE. April. What are you still doing here?

APRIL. I was working late with Mr. Shalimar. We drank Scotch, and he ordered up steaks to eat.

CAROLINE. Steak in the office?

APRIL. Yes. I ate all of mine and his too! He said he wasn't hungry, and he just kept drinking Scotch. *(Dreamy, like she's back in Mr. Shalimar's office.)* I was looking out of the window at all of the tall buildings thinking, here I am, April Morrison, part of it. And Mr. Shalimar grabbed me. He tried to kiss me!

CAROLINE. What did you do?

APRIL. I didn't know what to do. I just yelled *(Loud.)* "MR. SHALIMAR!" It sounded so stupid.

CAROLINE. Was he angry?

APRIL. No. He just stood there, smiling at me. He said "Oh, it wasn't as bad as all that." And then he gave me two dollars for cab fare.

CAROLINE. You shouldn't stay late with him. You could get into trouble.

APRIL. Do you think so?

CAROLINE. I do.

APRIL. I suppose you're right. *(Beat.)* You're here late too. Don't you have plans tonight?

CAROLINE. None. *(Beat.)* I've been dreading the weekend, having time to think about Eddie.

APRIL. Was that the boy you were engaged to?

CAROLINE. Yes. Eddie Harris. When the week began I was just so relieved to have eight less hours a day to think about him. But now — I wonder what it's like to be Miss Farrow? She certainly doesn't have to worry about having her heart broken.

APRIL. I wonder if you could have Miss Farrow's life without being mean like Miss Farrow?

CAROLINE. I'd like to find out.

APRIL You're so ambitious!

CAROLINE. Well, a girl has to do something.

APRIL. *(Blurts out.)* Caroline, are you a virgin?

CAROLINE. Pardon?

APRIL. *(Embarrassed.)* Never mind. I'm sorry. Sometimes I act like the most terrible hick.

CAROLINE. It's all right. I must admit, I am a virgin.

APRIL. Oh, sure. What do you mean "admit"? None of back home will admit they aren't.

CAROLINE. I'm not so proud of it. It's just something I can't bring myself to give up. If my mother heard me talking about in such a casual way she'd have a fit. She taught me only two rules for life: One, don't let boys touch you. Two, join the Radcliffe Club.

APRIL. My mother would no more tell me not to sleep with a boy than she would tell me not to go out and steal a car. She knows I wouldn't think of it.

CAROLINE. But you do think of it?

APRIL. I think *about* it. All the time. That's a little different though.

CAROLINE. When I'm twenty-six, if I'm not married by then, I'm going to take a lover.

APRIL. *(Shocked.)* Really?

CAROLINE. Yes!

APRIL. I think you're right. If you're that old, you have a right to live.

CAROLINE. I wanted to sleep with Eddie, but at the last minute I was always afraid. Of course I was afraid that I'd lose him if I went all the way.

APRIL. Of course.

CAROLINE. But I was also scared that going all the way wasn't going to be as wonderful as everything I'd always imagined.

APRIL. I guess this sounds awfully naive. But when I try to picture going to bed with somebody I can never figure out where the sheet and blankets go. Do you do it underneath the blanket, or do you take the blanket off —

CAROLINE. Didn't you ever neck on a bed with somebody?

APRIL. *(Scandalized.)* My heavens no. Not on a bed.

CAROLINE. Well, when the time comes, whoever he is, he'll know what to do about the blanket.

APRIL. What if you didn't wait until you were twenty-six? What if you were to take a lover next week? Just pretend — who would you want it to be? What kind of man would you want for your first? Do you know?

CAROLINE. This is just pretend, right?

APRIL. Of course.

CAROLINE. Mr. Rice.

19

APRIL. Mr. Rice from *The Cross*?

CAROLINE. He's so interesting. He's not like the boys I've met before. He's a man.

APRIL. I wish that I would meet a boy who would take me out to dinner and be good to me. Oh, who am I kidding, he wouldn't even have to take me to dinner.

CAROLINE. How else will you eat on $50 a week?

APRIL. There are so many things I'd like to talk to you about. Do you have to go back to the Port Blair tonight? Why don't you stay with me in my apartment?

CAROLINE. It would be exciting to spend the whole night in the city.

APRIL. Wait until you see my place. It's a dump, but I love it. I have a bed in the wall. There's one closet — the other closet is the kitchen. And I have a garden just three floors down. I'm not allowed to go in it, but I can look at it from my window.

CAROLINE. It sounds wonderful. I would love to live in the city. Maybe if I become a reader I can convince my parents to let me do it. *(From offstage we hear Gregg Adams singing something like "Life is Just a Bowl of Cherries."* When she enters the lights shift and a band kicks in. It feels like we're in a nightclub and Gregg is the star act. The songs ends with a big musical flourish! April and Caroline applaud. Then the lights shift abruptly, and we're back at the office.)* Are you Gregg Adams?

GREGG. Why yes.

CAROLINE. Mary Agnes said you're an actress.

GREGG. Mary Agnes Russo, the Louella Parsons of the 35th floor.

APRIL. I'm April Morrison and this is Caroline Bender. We just started this week.

GREGG. Terrific! I wasn't expecting a party.

CAROLINE. Do you usually report for work at 11 P.M. on Friday?

GREGG. I was on my way home and I thought I'd grab a nightcap. *(The lights shift to something ominous as melodramatic underscoring comes up and builds to a crescendo under Gregg's monologue. This feels like a cinematic close-up.)* Sometimes when I'm alone in my apartment I feel this stifling sensation creeping up on me. It's like a ten-pound weight is on my chest and I'm hardly able to breathe. You could die in New York behind the locked door of your apartment and no one would ever know until some neighbor complained of

* See Special Note on Songs and Recordings on copyright page.

20

the smell. *(The underscoring reaches a crescendo. Then the music cuts out and lights shift as though none of this had happened. She heads to Mr. Shalimar's office and calls out from offstage.)* This is the best bar in town when you're short of funds. Which, when you're me, is always. *(She returns brandishing a bottle of Scotch and some cups.)* I knew Shalimar wouldn't let me down.

CAROLINE. None for me, thanks.

APRIL. I don't think we should drink Mr. Shalimar's Scotch.

GREGG. I've been doing this since I started working here. He never notices. He has about fifty bottles under his desk.

APRIL. Gregg, what kind of an actress are you?

GREGG. Last week I had twelve lines in a morning soap opera and they promised me more in the future. And I did a commercial where I play a teenager and say *(With a slight Texan accent.)* "Gee, Mom this tastes like more!"

CAROLINE. What's that accent?

GREGG. I'm from Dallas. But I grew up in boarding schools around here. My parents were each other's second marriages and then they got divorced and remarried, so they didn't really want me around for very long.

CAROLINE. Did you know Helen Lowe in Dallas?

GREGG. Sure, the Lowes own Dallas. How do you know Helen?

CAROLINE. She married a boy I knew. Actually he was the boy I was supposed to marry.

GREGG. I heard Helen got herself a handsome Harvard boy.

CAROLINE. Yes. Eddie is handsome. He plays jazz piano and reads Fitzgerald and has a wonderful sense of humor.

APRIL. Oh, Caroline.

GREGG. The most attractive thing about Helen is her father's oil wells.

CAROLINE. Maybe I overestimated him. Eddie didn't have a job after graduation — I suppose he thought marrying oil wells would solve everything.

GREGG. You're better off. My sister married her college sweetheart and that was three husbands ago.

APRIL. *Three* husbands?

GREGG. We're not a very faithful family. Except me. I've got all the glue they forgot to hand out to the rest of them. When I get married I'm going to stay married. I've been saying goodbye to people all my life, and I'm sick of it. *(She lights a cigarette.)* Girls, I have met the most

21

wonderful man tonight. Have you heard of David Wilder Savage?

CAROLINE. The boy wonder of Broadway? Sure.

APRIL. I read about him in *Unveiled* magazine. Every play he produced was a success.

CAROLINE. Except that last one.

APRIL. His college roommate wrote that play.

GREGG. Gordon McKay. He was killed in an automobile crash.

APRIL. It said in *Unveiled* that there were rumors about them. That no one knows for sure whether they were in love with each other. I didn't know what that meant. They're boys!

GREGG. Well, I happen to know it's a lie.

CAROLINE. How?

GREGG. Because he made love to me.

CAROLINE. He wouldn't do that if he didn't like women.

APRIL. Gregg, what was it like?

GREGG. I was at this cocktail party, and I saw him there. *(Music, preferably something with bongos. Lights shift and we're at the party. David Wilder Savage enters, wearing a smoking jacket. Caroline and April watch the following exchange.)* I'm trying to think of something to say besides "Hello I'm an actress," and he looks at *me* and says:

DAVID WILDER SAVAGE. *(Hot.)* Who the hell are you?

GREGG. Gregg Adams.

DAVID WILDER SAVAGE. You look like a parolee from a boarding school.

GREGG. I was once.

DAVID WILDER SAVAGE. *(Moving closer.)* Have you read a book called *Many Faces?* It's Portuguese.

GREGG. I read the reviews.

DAVID WILDER SAVAGE. Come uptown to my house. I want to make love to you. *(Gregg and David move closer to each other.)*

GREGG. *(To the girls.)* He took off my dress and slip and stockings without ever removing his lips from my mouth and face.

CAROLINE. He *is* a boy wonder. *(Lights shift. David Wilder Savage straightens his smoking jacket and exits. The girls all watch him go. Music out.)*

APRIL. Gregg. What if you get … pregnant?

GREGG. There was a little rubber sixteenth of an inch between me and the Home for Unwed Mothers. I made sure of that. And he said next time I have to contribute. So there's going to be a next time!

APRIL. That's wonderful!

CAROLINE. So why did you leave?

GREGG. He has some silly rule that no girl is ever allowed to spend the entire night in his apartment. But before I left, I told him that I thought I loved him. And he took me in his arms and kissed me.

APRIL. Gregg, I think I will have a little Scotch please.

CAROLINE. Maybe we should go to The Unfriendly Irishman. Find someone to buy us a drink.

APRIL. Someone like Mr. Rice?

CAROLINE. Perhaps.

GREGG. I'm game. Let's get out of this rat-trap. *(Caroline takes the manuscript and the reports. She looks out, excited.)*

CAROLINE. Let's go, girls. To the wolves.

## Scene 3

*One month later. Caroline is in Mike Rice's office.*

MIKE RICE. I have a proposal for you.

CAROLINE. A proposal, Mr. Rice? *(He pours himself a drink.)* Why do you drink so much?

MIKE RICE. I like whisky. I prefer it to people. No problems, no responsibilities, no reproaches. Take you and me, for instance. I woke up this morning, and as usual I was thinking about you. And all of a sudden I knew I was in love with you.

CAROLINE. What did you do then?

MIKE RICE. I got out of bed and found a towel.

CAROLINE. *(Embarrassed and touched.)* Oh, you're terrible!

MIKE RICE. Then I went back to bed and thought about you some more.

CAROLINE. What a way to talk.

MIKE RICE. I want to have an affair with you. But I think it would ruin your life. Let's have a strange, private love affair all our own. A vicarious, mental affair.

CAROLINE. What's that?

MIKE RICE. We'll be absolutely honest with each other. I'll tell you everything I want to do to you, and you'll tell me everything you want to do to me.

CAROLINE. *(Confused.)* Do to you? *(Realizing.)* Oh!

MIKE RICE. We'll think of each other at the same time every night, before we go to sleep. We'll have a real affair of the heart.

CAROLINE. *(Bold.)* Why not just have a real affair?

MIKE RICE. Because you have your youth and your future, and I have my mind and my bottle. That's no trade, Caroline, the harm is all to you and the gain is all to me. That's all I'm concerned about. Not hurting you.

CAROLINE. I care very much about what happens to you. *(He takes her hand and they look at each other.)*

MIKE RICE. So tonight, we'll meet at the water cooler at 5 P.M.

CAROLINE. As usual.

MIKE RICE. We'll go downstairs for our regular drink. At 11 o'clock we'll go home and get into bed. At 11:30, I'll think about you, and you'll think about me. Okay?

CAROLINE. What should I *do*?

MIKE RICE. *(Seductive.)* Whatever you want.

CAROLINE. I should get back to my desk. Miss Farrow is probably having kittens. *(Caroline retreats to her desk. In the typing pool, Brenda is brandishing a white lace nightgown. Caroline notices.)* Something new for the trousseau?

BRENDA. Can you believe how darling?

MARY AGNES. You must have forty-five nightgowns by now!

BRENDA. It's a lot of work. But once a girl is married she has to be prepared.

MARY AGNES. Don't you feel strange about having a double bed? When I go to visit my girlfriends who are married now, and I see their bedroom, it's almost like they're saying "Now you know what *we* do." *(The phone rings and Brenda answers. Caroline gets to work, but Mary Agnes listens closely.)*

BRENDA. Hello, Mother. No. We're serving peas *and* mashed potatoes at the reception. Mother, nobody likes string beans. *(Notices Mary Agnes.)* Excuse me. *(Brenda returns to her call. Mary Agnes heads off.)*

MARY AGNES. Honestly, this is a place of business, not a sorority house! *(Miss Farrow storms in and heads for Caroline.)*

AMANDA. Mr. Shalimar tells me you've been reading manuscripts for him.

CAROLINE. I —

AMANDA. Did you think I wouldn't find out?

CAROLINE. Mr. Shalimar asked me. He said —

AMANDA. This explains why your secretarial duties, the duties you are being paid to perform, have been so utterly below par.

CAROLINE. I wasn't aware you felt that way, Miss Farrow.

AMANDA. Well, now you know. As does Mr. Shalimar.

CAROLINE. I've been trying to do a good job.

AMANDA. What you have been trying to do, Miss Bender, is to ingratiate yourself with Mr. Shalimar, to go over my head and deceive me, and to attempt to show that you know more than I do after my 15 years in this business.

CAROLINE. I just wanted the opportunity to do more —

AMANDA. Listen, you little bitch. I am an editor. You think you're a reader, but you are just another typist. Don't you forget it. *(Miss Farrow exits. Caroline is stunned. Mary Agnes enters.)*

MARY AGNES. What did she say? You look like she hit you in the face.

CAROLINE. I think … I think she said I'm going to be a reader after all.


## Scene 4


*It's the Tuesday before Christmas — the day of the Fabian Christmas Party. One of the manuscript tables is holding a box filled with decorations, and there's a fully stocked bar on one of the desks. April is there, looking very fashionable.*

*Caroline and Gregg enter, dressed up a bit for the party.*


APRIL. Merry Christmas!

CAROLINE. Merry Christmas!

GREGG. Bah Humbug.

CAROLINE. Oh stop. You should see what she's done to our apartment. It looks like a window at Gimbels.

APRIL. That apartment is so darling. With the studio couches and everything. *(Brenda and Mary Agnes enter, both in extremely*

*festive attire.)*
MARY AGNES. Merry Christmas, girls! Gee, aren't you going to get dressed up for the Christmas party?
CAROLINE. We are dressed up.
MARY AGNES. *(Trying to be kind. Failing.)* Oh. *(Miss Farrow's phone rings. April answers.)*
APRIL. Miss Farrow's office. Oh hello, Miss Farrow. Yes it's all taken care of. Oh, alright then. Yes. Merry *(Looks at receiver.)* Christmas. *(Looks at the girls.)* Miss Farrow's not coming to the office party.
MARY AGNES. She never comes. She considers the whole thing a waste of time and she takes the day off on the grounds that she deserves it.
APRIL. That's a relief! I know *I* deserve it.
CAROLINE. You are doing a wonderful job April. Much better than I did.
APRIL. It's not so unpleasant right now. I've spent most of my days in the department stores purchasing her Christmas list. I sent presents to her whole family back home in Racine, Wisconsin. And I bought two presents she wants to deliver herself — a man's smoking jacket *and* a man's silk bathrobe.
CAROLINE. No one would buy a smoking jacket and a silk bathrobe for the same man at the same time.
GREGG. Mr. Bossart must have a rival.
MARY AGNES. *(Gasps.)* Do you think one is for Mr. Bossart?
CAROLINE. If they're lovers, then I think she'd give him a Christmas present.
BRENDA. Sure, so she gets something in return. *(Brenda puts her wedding album on the desk and opens it with a flourish.)* Well. Have you all seen my wedding album?
GREGG. Gee, and here I thought this party would be boring.
BRENDA. I thought they didn't allow temps at this party.
GREGG. They don't. But this is my swan song. I quit!
CAROLINE. You do?
GREGG. I was going to tell you at our apartment this morning, but there just wasn't time. David got me that job. I'll be the ingenue in at least four plays. Real United States money. So I'm still good for my share of the rent, even though I'll be in Connecticut.
CAROLINE. Connecticut?
APRIL. *(Turning a page in Brenda's album.)* Oh. That cake looks

delicious!

BRENDA. I never even got a bite, but everyone else love
tiers! *America's Woman* did a photo shoot of wedding cak
got Barbara LeMont to get me a discount. She won't need it. *(*
*Agnes updates the other girls.)*

MARY AGNES. Barbara LeMont is divorced. And she has a litt
girl. It's terrible. I don't know what I'd do if Bill and I got divorced. I can't imagine not knowing I was going to be married
soon. *(Caroline, Gregg and April look at each other.)* I'm sorry,
girls!

BRENDA. You'll find somebody. Don't you worry.

GREGG. I've got somebody.

CAROLINE. I'm not worried. *(Gregg and Caroline clink glasses.)*

MARY AGNES. I admire you. Most girls our age are scared to
death if there's nobody on the horizon, and that's silly. Because if
you look at the girls five years older than we are, why, I don't know
one who isn't married.

CAROLINE. I do.

APRIL. Are they terribly ugly?

CAROLINE. Quite the contrary. I've met some at parties who are
very pretty and smart, too, with good jobs.

MARY AGNES. *(Philosophical.)* Well, perhaps there's something
psychologically wrong with them.

BRENDA. I'm going to ask Mr. Shalimar if we can start the
music.

MARY AGNES. I should come with you. Last year when I went
in there alone he tried to kiss me right on the mouth. *(She starts to
exit and Brenda follows.)*

BRENDA. Mr. Shalimar is an old garter-snapper.

MARY AGNES. I didn't like it.

CAROLINE. When did I become the pathetic figure of the
unattached girl?

APRIL. Maybe you'll meet someone today. I heard that boys from
all the banks sneak into the Fabian party, because we have the best-
looking secretaries.

CAROLINE. I hope they're better than the Fabian men.

GREGG. They're nearly all married, aren't they? Married or
Queersville or so young and poor they'd hardly be able to take you
to the Automat.

CAROLINE. Or so dull. It's as if they're just suits suspended from

..sible shoulders, looking for the right kind of wife. At Radcliffe we called it Gracious Living.

APRIL. What about Mr. Rice?

CAROLINE. He's not Gracious Living, that's for certain.

GREGG. No. Gracious Living isn't saying naughty things to do to each other on the phone every night.

CAROLINE. *(Embarrassed.)* Gregg!

GREGG. I sleep on the other side of the room.

CAROLINE. You're never even there!

GREGG. Remember the other night when David was away and I fell asleep early? In the morning you asked me if I heard anything? Well, I heard *anything*.

APRIL. It's like the Fabian paperback I'm reading, *Babylon Road*.

CAROLINE. You're reading *that?*

APRIL. Oh yes. It's about a chaste young nun and the priest she loves. They whisper to each other at night through the convent walls, but they never consummate the relationship. It's very romantic.

GREGG. That's sounds like my kind of book. Let me borrow it when you're finished. *(Brenda enters.)*

BRENDA. Mr. Shalimar said we could start the music. Come on boys. *(Music up. All of the girls — except for Caroline--bring on identical Man in the Grey Flannel Suit cardboard cutouts. They are flat and man-shaped and very two-dimensional. It's a Dance Break! The girls lindy hop with the cutouts. At some point in the dance, the cutouts surround Caroline, vying for her attention. She is not interested, and even a little threatened. The girls pair off around the stage with the cutouts. April approaches Caroline, holding her cutout. The music should continue under the dialogue.)*

APRIL. I've met the most interesting boy. Dexter Key. Isn't that a wonderful name? It sounds so social. He works at Merrill Lynch Pierce Fenner and Beane.

CAROLINE. Impressive.

APRIL. Caroline, he's going to take me to Sardi's!

CAROLINE. Have fun, April. And have wonderful holidays with your family in Colorado.

APRIL. Merry Christmas! Happy New Year! *(The music comes back up in full and April and the other girls finish the dance. As they leave, Mike Rice enters. He is NOT in a grey flannel suit. Music changes to something more sultry, maybe a rhumba. Mike Rice leans over and kisses Caroline very lightly on the lips.)*

MIKE RICE.  Did you think of me last night?

CAROLINE.  Yes.

MIKE RICE.  What did you do?

CAROLINE.  I thought of you in your dismal hotel. I thought of how I feel about you — as a person, a companion, my dearest friend. I went to sleep, and I dreamed of you. If it's possible to say that one mind is sleeping with another mind, then that's what we're doing.

MIKE RICE.  Anything is possible. Tell me what you want me to do to you.

CAROLINE.  You know I hate to talk that way.

MIKE RICE.  Tell me. How else will I know? Do you want me to kiss you?

CAROLINE.  Yes.

MIKE RICE.  Then say so.

CAROLINE.  I want you to kiss me. And you never do! Just good night, like an old uncle. *(Mike leans over and kisses her. Like an old uncle.)*

CAROLINE.  There you go again.

MIKE RICE.  If I started to kiss you — really kiss you — I couldn't stop there. *(They look at each other. The tension is thick.)* I'll get you a drink. Don't you want one? *(She doesn't answer.)* I do, in any case. *(He starts to go. Caroline steps in front of him.)*

CAROLINE.  Mike.

MIKE RICE.  Yes, Caroline.

CAROLINE.  There is something I want you to do.

MIKE RICE.  Tell me.

CAROLINE.  Please. Please. Sleep with me.

# Scene 5

*Two weeks later. The office has been closed over the holiday break. Caroline is in the elevator, which can be indicated with lights and sound. It's very early, well before anyone else is usually in the office, but Mike Rice steps in. It is extremely awkward.*

MIKE RICE. Well. Happy New Year.

CAROLINE. Happy New Year. *(The elevator door closes. They are quiet and very uncomfortable as the elevator continues to the 35th floor — Fabian.)*

MIKE RICE. Nice holidays?

CAROLINE. Yes. You?

MIKE RICE. Yes. *(Ding! A long pause. Finally, Ding! They arrive at Fabian and step out.)* So here it is. The awkward first encounter after you've been to bed together before the Christmas break.

CAROLINE. Been to bed together. That sounds very sophisticated.

MIKE RICE. Caroline. I'm sorry I disappointed you.

CAROLINE. It's all right. I was glad you stopped.

MIKE RICE. I was hurting you. I couldn't bear it.

CAROLINE. I know. Mike, you were right. It was an impossible situation. I was too much of a schoolgirl to see it. But now I do.

MIKE RICE. *(Hurt.)* Oh. Good. Good. Then, we'll go for a drink tonight. Surround ourselves with people we once thought were absurd bores.

CAROLINE. Darling. Not tonight.

MIKE RICE. Oh?

CAROLINE. My New Year's resolution is to get to those damn Westerns I've been putting off reading. If I can find something worthy maybe I'll be on my way to becoming an editor.

MIKE RICE. I see.

CAROLINE. Happy New Year. *(Caroline kisses him on his forehead, like an old uncle, and heads to her cubicle. Mike watches her go.)*

## Scene 6

*Two weeks later. Caroline and April are in Caroline's cubicle.*

APRIL.  Do I look different to you?

CAROLINE.  Different?

APRIL.  I've been wanting to tell you ever since it happened. But how can you just tell somebody?

CAROLINE.  What is it? Is it something to do with Dexter?

APRIL.  We've been sleeping together for two whole weeks! Are you shocked?

CAROLINE.  No.

APRIL.  Remember how I was trying to figure out whether you did it under the sheets or on top of them?

CAROLINE.  Yes.

APRIL.  Well, the first time — right in the middle of it — I suddenly thought to myself, now I know. I must tell Caroline.

CAROLINE.  *That's* what you thought about?

APRIL.  I guess people think funny things the first time.

CAROLINE.  I guess so.

APRIL.  With Dexter, I feel so different than when I first came here. I feel like I belong.

CAROLINE.  That's how I feel about work.

APRIL.  About work?

CAROLINE.  April, I've decided. I'm going to be an editor.

APRIL.  Miss Farrow will hate that!

CAROLINE.  I'm doing the work. And I need the money.

APRIL.  But you have your own cubicle!

CAROLINE.  A cubicle isn't an office. *(Miss Farrow enters. She's not wearing her hat.)*

APRIL.  I was just going back to my desk, Miss Farrow.

AMANDA.  *(Offhand.)* Fine.

APRIL.  See you later, Caroline. *(April exits. Caroline sits at her desk.)*

AMANDA.  You'll have time to read these, won't you? *(She pushes a pile of dusty manuscripts towards Caroline.)*

CAROLINE. What are they?

AMANDA. I'm cleaning out my backlog. I'm leaving on Friday.

CAROLINE. Leaving!

AMANDA. There will be a memo going around to that effect.

CAROLINE. *(Unsure what to say.)* This must be quite a shock to everyone.

AMANDA. I don't like to go in such a hurry and leave you all up in the air. But it can't be helped.

CAROLINE. Where ... are you going?

AMANDA. *(Smiling.)* I'm getting married.

CAROLINE. Married? You?

AMANDA. My fiancé is moving his plant to California. So of course I have to leave Fabian.

CAROLINE. *(Recovering her manners.)* How exciting! I certainly wish you all the luck in the world.

AMANDA. Thank you.

CAROLINE. We'll miss you.

AMANDA. Well. *(A moment. She hands over a list.)* Here is a list of my authors and the manuscripts some of them are working on. *(Caroline takes the paper carefully, like it's a rare original document.)*

CAROLINE. Thank you. Some of these are the pick of the crop.

AMANDA. Yes. They've been with me for many years. I've decided to give them to you.

CAROLINE. I appreciate that, Miss Farrow.

AMANDA. You should. You'll have to work hard. Twice as hard as the men. You'll have to keep a watch on what each of the writers are doing, encourage them, write to them if they haven't done anything for us in a while, edit their manuscripts, even listen to their troubles.

CAROLINE. I'd love that!

AMANDA. I think you will. Goodbye, Miss Bender. *(She starts to leave.)*

CAROLINE. I guess I'll need an expense account to take them to lunch.

AMANDA. You can discuss the details with Mr. Shalimar.

CAROLINE. I'm sure Mr. Shalimar will follow your recommendation.

AMANDA. An expense account should be fine.

CAROLINE. The same as yours. We don't want them to think they've been handed down to an assistant.

AMANDA. Mine is very small.

CAROLINE. *(Bluffing.)* I know what it is.

AMANDA. Well, then, of course you'll get the same.

CAROLINE. Thank you. *(Beat.)* Of course I'll be getting some kind of raise in accordance with my promotion.

AMANDA. Oh, I don't know about a raise. This new job is quite an honor for you.

CAROLINE. I don't expect to be paid as much as you. But twenty dollars a week seems a fair compromise.

AMANDA. The company isn't that rich. *(Beat.)* You'll get something. But I wouldn't count on twenty dollars.

CAROLINE. Fine.

AMANDA. *(Impressed.)* I'll convey all of this to Mr. Shalimar. *(They shake hands, like two men. Miss Farrow looks closely at Caroline.)*

AMANDA. Miss Bender. Now that you're a real editor, get yourself a hat.


## Scene 7


*Mary Agnes's bridal shower! The typing pool is decorated a little and Mary Agnes is wearing a corsage.*


MARY AGNES. We're going to Bermuda for the honeymoon. The beaches are pink. And people wear long shorts and ride bicycles. I've never ridden a bicycle, but Bill says he can teach me. I just hope I don't get too sunburned.

BRENDA. Oh, I don't think you'll have much opportunity to get a sunburn. You'll be lucky to leave your hotel room. *(Mary Agnes is mortified. Brenda pulls herself up and she is hugely pregnant. She walks over to the bar.)* I'm dying for more champagne. *(She pours herself a big glass.)*

MARY AGNES. We're having a bottle of liquor on each table. And we ordered four whole cases of champagne!

BRENDA. A bottle on every table? That's a bit much.

MARY AGNES. *(As though Brenda had asked a question.)* For dinner we're having little rolls, fruit cup, soup, chicken and string beans and potatoes lyonnais, salad, ice cream and wedding cake.

APRIL. It sounds awfully delicious, Mary Agnes.

BRENDA. That's a lot of food. People are going to get sick. *(Caroline enters.)*

MARY AGNES. Caroline! You came!

BRENDA. And only an hour late.

CAROLINE. I had a lunch meeting.

APRIL. Mary Agnes was just telling us all about the wedding plans.

CAROLINE. Is there booze? *(Brenda points. Caroline pours herself a large glass of Scotch.)*

APRIL. Mary Agnes, your ring is beautiful.

MARY AGNES. I picked it out together with the wedding ring and groom's ring. They all match. I saw them in this advertisement and I knew they were perfect. *(She picks up* America's Woman *magazine. The girls all look.)*

BRENDA. *(With awe.)* "A Diamond is Forever." I love that.

CAROLINE. It's brilliant. Do you know the woman who wrote that copy isn't even married?

MARY AGNES. That's so sad. She probably doesn't even own a diamond.

APRIL. You picked the ring out yourself? You didn't want it to be a surprise?

MARY AGNES. Well, I knew exactly the ring I wanted. We've both been saving for so long. It just seemed silly. *(Brenda holds up her be-ringed finger.)*

BRENDA. I showed Lenny's sister the ring I wanted. And then I told her exactly how he should propose — take me to dinner at Luzio's, hire a violinist, and get on his knee in the middle of the restaurant. And hold the ring out like this. *(She demonstrates.)*

APRIL. And that worked?

BRENDA. Sure. You've got to make it easy for them. They're not good at figuring it out on their own.

CAROLINE. But it wasn't a surprise.

BRENDA. Yeah but you can't just ask for a ring. That's crass.

APRIL. Mary Agnes, may I try your ring on please? If you don't have any special feeling for not taking it off, I mean.

MARY AGNES. I take it off at night when I go to bed. I always keep it in the little velvet box on my dresser. *(She hands the ring to April. April holds it for an instant, looking at it, then slips it on her*

34

*finger. She holds her hand out and looks at it. She mouths "Yes!")*

MARY AGNES. It fits you perfectly. I was afraid it'd be too small and then you'd never get it off.

BRENDA. Nah, we'd just cut her finger off.

APRIL. I'm going to take it. You cut my finger off. *(April, Mary Agnes and Brenda laugh. Caroline looks at April, concerned. April slips the ring off and hands it to Mary Agnes.)* Thank you. It's beautiful, Mary Agnes.

MARY AGNES. You're welcome. *(Looks at the ring back on her finger.)* We're having a photographer to take movies and stills, and a wedding cake with a bride and groom on top. And the single girls will get cake to take home and put under their pillow to sleep on.

APRIL. And then the man you dream about is the man you'll marry.

CAROLINE. *(Teasing.)* What if you have a nightmare?

BRENDA. Then you end up with a ruined piece of cake. *(Caroline raises her glass to Brenda.)* Okay, Mary Agnes, time for your present! *(Brenda hands Mary Agnes a wrapped gift. She unwraps it and looks inside. What she sees there is unbelievably shocking. The other girls all gather around and peer in.)* I got it in Greenwich Village.

MARY AGNES. *(Looking at her watch.)* Well. I have a fitting for my dress! *(To Caroline and April.)* It's floor-length white satin with a high neckline, and a little tight-fitting waist and long sleeves that end in points and a long train and circles of lace with pearls.

BRENDA. I'm going to bring some cake to Barbara LeMont. *America's Woman* always has food left over from the photo shoots, and then I don't have to cook dinner. Last time I got a roast turkey! *(Brenda takes the cake and exits. Mary Agnes watches her go.)*

MARY AGNES. Three months pregnant, my eye! She's six months if she's a day, but she knows she has to quit at three months. And her husband is supposed to be so rich! I just feel embarrassed for her, walking around looking like that. *(She gathers up her things.)* Thank you for the lovely party girls! Don't stay here all night! Ha ha. *(Mary Agnes exits, holding the gift in front of her like she might catch something.)*

APRIL. Poor Mary Agnes. She's so frightened of what's going to happen at the honeymoon.

CAROLINE. It's a good thing she has the wedding to distract her from her marriage.

APRIL. Remember how she used to make fun of Brenda!

CAROLINE. At least she doesn't bring her underwear to the office.

APRIL. Caroline, can I tell you something?

CAROLINE. Of course. Is everything all right?

APRIL. Very all right. I am preparing for my wedding.

CAROLINE. *(Surprised.)* Why that's wonderful. So it's all set then?

APRIL. I've always felt that the wedding is mostly the girl's responsibility. I wrote to my relatives in Colorado to tell them to expect the good news any time now and to find out when the church would be available. And I made an appointment to try on dresses at Saks tomorrow. Would you come with me?

CAROLINE. I think you should wait until you and Dexter have finalized the details.

APRIL. Oh Caroline, you don't know him. He hates to be bothered about these things. If I arrange everything, he'll be so glad. Did I show you what he gave me? *(April shows Caroline her necklace, a gold heart on a fragile chain.)*

CAROLINE. It's lovely.

APRIL. He just gave it to me, it wasn't even Christmas or my birthday or anything! A heart means love.

CAROLINE. It doesn't mean you're engaged.

APRIL. I met his parents. His mother invited me to lunch.

CAROLINE. April. When people are engaged, they make plans together. That's what Eddie and I did.

APRIL. Well that didn't work out at all!

CAROLINE. *(Hurt.)* No it didn't. But I know boys like Dexter. You're going to get hurt.

APRIL. Caroline, I'm not like you. I don't want to be alone. I want to get married.

CAROLINE. *(Hurt.)* I want to get married.

APRIL. You just work work work. You're like Miss Farrow. And even she got married! If any boy has the nerve to like you, you make fun of him. I may be a stupid farm girl, but I love Dexter and he loves me. I'm going to marry him and we're going to be happy forever and I'm going to have everything I want! *(April faints.)*

## Scene 8

*Two weeks later. Caroline's office, after hours. Caroline mixes orange juice, Scotch and gin in a large glass and hands it to April.*

CAROLINE. This is the special Harvard Weekend punch. You don't even taste the gin, and then — boom! You're blind. *(April smiles weakly.)* More innocent girls have been seduced as a result of this punch than you could imagine. You won't even want an anesthetic.

APRIL. Dexter said they don't give you an anesthetic. He said it's because if the police come we have to run.

CAROLINE. That won't happen. You're not doing anything wrong, April.

APRIL. I'm breaking the law!

CAROLINE. *(Uncertain.)* Well. It's a bad law. Now drink.

APRIL. *(Drinks.)* I have a picture in my mind of a dried-up little man in a doctor's white jacket. He's going to hate me.

CAROLINE. No. He won't.

APRIL. You would never have let this happen to you.

CAROLINE. That doesn't matter.

APRIL. Dexter said we could get married in the spring.

CAROLINE. Is that what you want?

APRIL. I wanted to have this baby. *(Beat.)* But it's all arranged.

CAROLINE. It will be all right. All of your friends love you. I love you.

APRIL. People die from abortions. *(Caroline doesn't know what to say.)*

CAROLINE. You're going to be fine. And afterward Dexter will bring you to my apartment and you'll sleep all weekend and I'll wait on you hand and foot.

APRIL. Yes. Dexter wouldn't take me to a bad place. He knows about these things.

CAROLINE. *(Bitter.)* Yes, I'm sure he does.

APRIL. *(Defensive.)* It's a real doctor. In New Jersey. Dexter only knows about him from one of his friends who got his girl into

37

trouble. And they got married a year later!

CAROLINE. Well then.

APRIL. What time is it? *(Caroline looks at her watch.)*

CAROLINE. Five o'clock.

APRIL. Dexter will be downstairs with the car. *(She hugs Caroline.)* Thank you. *(April faces the door and takes a breath. Then she walks slowly to the door.)*


## Scene 9


*Almost a year has passed.*

*Romantic music swells as lights come up on Caroline, asleep at her desk. Eddie Harris enters. He is standing very far away, and he's wearing a cowboy hat. The music underscores this entire scene, and it all feels pretty fantastical.*


EDDIE. Hello, Caroline.

CAROLINE. *(Groggy.)* Eddie? What are you doing here?

EDDIE. You're dreaming.

CAROLINE. Oh! *(Looks around.)* But I'm at work.

EDDIE. You're always at work.

CAROLINE. I'm an editor. *(Proud.)* The only female editor at Fabian Paperbacks. But I'd throw it away in a minute for a life as your wife.

EDDIE. You wouldn't have to. I'm proud of you. I'd like you to work, if that's what you want.

CAROLINE. Yes! Yes, I'd like to have both.

EDDIE. I love you, Caroline. I always have. I finally had to face it. *(He takes his cowboy hat off and puts her hat on. He leaves as the lights fade.)*

# Scene 10

*Later that week. Caroline's office. Mary Agnes appears in the doorway wearing a matronly-looking dress.*

MARY AGNES. Hi. Anybody home?

CAROLINE. Mary Agnes! It's been such a long time.

MARY AGNES. One whole year. I can't believe it. Did you get my birth announcement?

CAROLINE. I did, a little boy. Congratulations!

MARY AGNES. Thank you. How are you, Caroline?

CAROLINE. I've signed some wonderful authors. Bradley Everheart left his publisher to work with me.

MARY AGNES. You always were ambitious.

CAROLINE. I like this job.

MARY AGNES. *(She opens her purse and takes out an envelope of photos.)* Well. Look what *I've* got. Here's my *baby!* (Caroline looks through the first four of the bunch.)

CAROLINE. Oh, how cute. *(She starts to hand them back to Mary Agnes.)*

MARY AGNES. Take your time, look at all of them. *(April enters. She's more stylish and beautiful than ever, but she's wearing a lot of makeup to cover the dark circles under her eyes.)*

APRIL. Save me! I just agreed to a blind date. Hey it's Mary Agnes!

CAROLINE. *(A warning.)* We were just looking at pictures of Mary Agnes' baby. *(Mary Agnes takes one of the pictures from Caroline and holds it out to April.)*

APRIL. Crazy! Ronnie Wood from Springs, Colorado, called me from the pay phone across the street. His Aunt is a friend of my mother's, and he sounds like a real square. I told him I'd meet him for cocktails, get it over with before I have dinner with Walter.

MARY AGNES. Is Walter your boyfriend?

APRIL. Oh no! Walter's a gas, he's wild about me. I met him a couple of times through Tom.

CAROLINE. Tom had the private plane?

APRIL. Yes.

CAROLINE. *(To Mary Agnes.)* April has a new romance every month.

APRIL. If you're not having fun you might as well just give up and die.

MARY AGNES. You girls are so interesting. I was just over at *America's Woman* magazine to see Barbara Lemont, and she wasn't there! She eloped with Sidney Carter from the Sidney Carter agency and now she's going to stay home and take care of her little girl.

CAROLINE. His own agency? How old is he?

MARY AGNES. Forty. But he's terribly handsome.

APRIL. Why didn't an eighteen-karat man like that get grabbed up before?

MARY AGNES. He just got divorced. It's just too bad he's so old. But I suppose she's lucky to have gotten someone at all, with such a big child and everything.

CAROLINE. It's not the same here without you, Mary Agnes.

MARY AGNES. *(Wistful.)* I never liked working. I couldn't wait to get married and have a baby so I could quit. But now I miss it a little. Talking to you girls. *(She gets up, reluctantly.)* I should probably get going home. My mother doesn't like to be alone with the baby for very long.

CAROLINE. Would you like to take some books?

MARY AGNES. Books? Oh no. By the time I feed him and bathe him and wash and bleach his diapers and make dinner for Bill, it's all I can do to fall asleep in front of the television. You'll see. *(She walks to the window, emotional.)* Look at that view. I never noticed it when I worked here.*(She takes a moment. Then pulls herself together.)* I'll be seeing you. So long, girls. *(Mary Agnes exits.)*

APRIL. What a drag.

CAROLINE. At least she has something to do tonight.

APRIL. Sure, wash and bleach diapers.

CAROLINE. But she'll be with her husband and baby. Not eating a sandwich alone in an empty apartment because her roommate is never home.

APRIL. How is Gregg?

CAROLINE. She's acting peculiar. She calls David up all evening long. And then at about 12:30, just when I'm going to sleep, she leaves the house.

APRIL. I thought David wouldn't see her.

CAROLINE. He won't. I don't know where she goes.

APRIL. Poor Gregg. I know how she feels. Remember how strange I was when Dexter wouldn't see me anymore?

CAROLINE. Well, now you know better.

APRIL. I'm having an education. *(Beat.)* Caroline, will you tell me something?

CAROLINE. What?

APRIL. We'll count to three and then show each other how many fingers. Then neither of us will have to say it.

CAROLINE. Say what?

APRIL. How many boys we've slept with.

CAROLINE. All right.

APRIL. One, two, three, go! *(Caroline holds out one finger. April holds out four.)*

APRIL. Oh, I feel terrible. *(Ronnie Wood looks in. He has an Argoflex camera in a tan leather case over his shoulder, and he's wearing a Dacron suit, the kind you used to be able to wash out yourself in your hotel room.)*

RONNIE. Excuse me. I'm sorry to interrupt. *(He stammers.)* I'm, I'm looking for April Morrison?

APRIL. Hello Ronnie Wood.

RONNIE. *(Immediately smitten.)* April?

APRIL. Yes.

RONNIE. Wow. I'm glad to meet you. I'm glad you could make it tonight.

APRIL. This is my friend Caroline Bender.

RONNIE. *(Still looking at April.)* Hi.

APRIL. Where shall we go? Do you have a favorite place?

RONNIE. *(Stuttering.)* In New York City? Me? No … no. I thought … I'd leave it to you.

APRIL. For cocktails? The Barberry Room I guess. *(She notices Ronnie staring at her.)* What's the matter?

RONNIE. You're just. You look like everything a New York girl should be. Beautiful and poised and sophisticated. I wish … you'd have dinner with me.

APRIL. Well, maybe I can. Let's start with a martini okay? *(She gathers up her purse and coat and looks back at Caroline. Formal, being sophisticated.)* See you tomorrow, Caroline. Thank you for the talk.

CAROLINE. *(Smiling.)* Yes, April. Good night. *(Caroline watches them go. Music comes up. Caroline walks to the deserted typing pool and over to the filing cabinet. She pulls open a drawer, and there is the ship from the beginning of the play. She takes out the ship and examines it for a moment. As she exits we hear her in voiceover.)* Dear Eddie, It occurred to me that it has been almost two years since I last saw you. So many interesting things have happened to me since then ...


## Scene 11


*Three weeks later. Caroline's office. Caroline is looking through her mail. She buzzes her secretary, Lorraine.*


LORRAINE. *(Voiceover.)* Yes, Miss Bender?

CAROLINE. Lorraine, do you have any more of my mail?

LORRAINE. *(Voiceover.)* No, Miss Bender. I gave all of it to you.

CAROLINE. Please check with the mail room. I'm expecting something important from Texas.

LORRAINE. *(Voiceover.)* But Miss Bender, it's after 7 P.M. The mail room is closed.

CAROLINE. Oh. Of course.

LORRAINE. *(Voiceover.)* Do you need anything else tonight, Miss Bender?

CAROLINE. Did you type all of those reports for Mr. Shalimar?

LORRAINE. *(Voiceover.)* Yes.

CAROLINE. Then that's all. Good night, Lorraine. *(Caroline looks at her mail again, very carefully, hoping she missed a letter from Eddie. Nothing. She picks up a manuscript, and begins to read through it, making notes. Mr. Shalimar enters. He is very drunk.)*

MR. SHALIMAR. You're here late, Miss Bender. *(Caroline looks up from her work, startled.)*

MR. SHALIMAR. I hardly ever see you anymore. You must be avoiding me.

CAROLINE. I've just been working hard.

MR. SHALIMAR. All the same, you should come in to see me once in a while. I like to know what my favorite editors are doing. *(Caroline doesn't respond.)* Have you found any exciting new books for us?

CAROLINE. This manuscript I'm reading now may turn out to

be something.

MR. SHALIMAR. Good. Good. Keep at it. Keep turning them out. Are you enjoying the work, Miss Bender?

CAROLINE. I am. Very much.

MR. SHALIMAR. Here only two years and an editor. You're very ambitious. Very ambitious.

CAROLINE. I'm trying to do a good job.

MR. SHALIMAR. Little college girls walk in here and think they're going to tell everybody what to do. Think they can eat the world in three bites. Do you know how long it takes most people to be an editor?

CAROLINE. I've been very lucky Mr. Shalimar. *(Beat.)* Well, I was just on my way out — *(Caroline starts to leave, but Mr. Shalimar prevents her. This is subtle.)*

MR. SHALIMAR. You're skinny but you have a nice face. And you have nice legs. I love girls' legs. They're the most important part of a girl's body. Let me see your pretty legs. *(Caroline doesn't move.)* Then I'll see for myself. *(Mr. Shalimar lifts her skirt a bit and looks.)* You have beau-ti-ful legs! *(He tries to kiss Caroline. She moves away and he trips.)* You bitch. *(Caroline goes to him. She touches his shoulder.)*

CAROLINE. I love my job, Mr. Shalimar. All of your guidance has meant so much to me.

MR. SHALIMAR. That's all I ask, Miss Bender. Respect from my employees. *(He touches her face, then moves his hand to her breast. Caroline is frozen. Gregg enters, wearing a man's overcoat. The pockets of the coat are bulging, and she looks like she hasn't slept in weeks.)*

GREGG. Caroline. I went to the apartment but you weren't there.

CAROLINE. Gregg! *(She crosses to Gregg.)*

MR. SHALIMAR. Do come by my office for a visit sometime Miss Bender. *(He leaves. Caroline starts to button her blouse, shaken.)*

CAROLINE. Talk about a well-timed exit. You saved me.

GREGG. I found out who the girl was. There are two girls, but the second he likes better, and she goes there all the time now. The first one doesn't go there anymore.

CAROLINE. What are you talking about?

GREGG. David.

CAROLINE. Gregg, Mr. Shalimar just —

GREGG. The first night, when he threw me out, I stood outside of his door for a while. And hearing what he was doing, the sounds of his routine, it was almost as good as being there with him. *(Lights shift, and we're in David Wilder Savage's hallway.)* The stairway to the upper floor is just outside his door, and the wall it runs along is the outside wall to his apartment. In my mind I could see the layout of the rooms, and I knew it was his bedroom wall. *(She leans against the wall.)* I leaned against it. I could hear David's footsteps. It was so intimate. I've been going there at night after he goes to bed, and just listening. *(She listens.)* The girl asked if he minded if she slept on his side of the bed. She said she's peculiar that way. David thinks she might be compulsive. *(Lights shift back to Caroline's office. Gregg pulls her hands out of her pockets and holds out a pill bottle, a lipstick case, an empty cigarette pack.)* I found a bottle of pills with her name on it. I called the drugstore and pretended I was her and asked them to renew my prescription. But the druggist said it had codeine in it and he couldn't renew it. I think it was a painkiller, not a sleeping pill, because David has sleeping pills he could have given her. Isn't that funny — I know everything about her, what color lipstick she wears, how her voice sounds, what kind of cigarettes she smokes, how big her feet are, even when she has her period. And I've never seen her. She doesn't even know I know.

CAROLINE. Where did you find this stuff?

GREGG. His wastebasket. The maid puts all these things out in the back hall in a paper bag for the janitor to take away.

CAROLINE. Gregg, this isn't doing you any good. Why don't we get the trades? I'll bet there are some auditions you should go on.

GREGG. Her name is Judy. I think he likes her a lot.

CAROLINE. Listen to me. You need to stop this nonsense. When Eddie left me, I was upset, I was miserable. But I got this job, and I met you and April. I've accomplished so much that I never dreamed was possible. *(Gregg looks at Caroline. A penetrating look.)*

GREGG. Caroline. You're so smart.

CAROLINE. Gregg, I know you. You're not this person. *(Gregg touches Caroline's face.)*

GREGG. I wonder what she has that I didn't have? But don't worry. I'm going to find out.

# Scene 12

*Caroline's office, a few weeks later. Caroline is on the phone.*

CAROLINE. Look, I'm sorry about the *Unveiled* story. It's a piece of garbage. But Fabian Paperbacks are separate from that. *(She listens.)* John Cassaro is a big star. He should know better than to take an 18-year-old girl out to a place where they'll be photographed together. *(She listens.)* Listen, it's none of my business. I just need him to endorse the book. *(She listens.)* Wonderful. I'll bring the contracts to his hotel personally. Thank you. *(She hangs up the phone, looking pleased with herself. The intercom buzzes.)* Oh, Lorraine, I was just about to buzz you. Please prepare those contracts for Mr. Cassaro's signature. I'll bring them to him tomorrow.

LORRAINE. *(Voiceover.)* You're going to meet him in person? He's my favorite movie star!

CAROLINE. I'll get you an autograph.

LORRAINE.. *(Voiceover.)* Thank you, Miss Bender!

CAROLINE. You're welcome.

LORRAINE. *(Voiceover.)* Oh, Miss Bender, I almost forgot. Mr. Eddie Harris is here to see you. *(Caroline is speechless for a moment. Then.)*

CAROLINE. I'm sorry, Lorraine. What did you say?

LORRAINE. *(Voiceover.)* Mr. Eddie Harris. He doesn't have an appointment. But he said he's an old friend.

CAROLINE. Yes. Yes, of course. Send him back, Lorraine. *(Caroline tries to decide whether she should sit or stand. Eddie enters.)*

EDDIE. Hello, Caroline.

CAROLINE. Eddie.

EDDIE. I'm in town for a few days on business. I thought I could take you to lunch.

CAROLINE. Lunch?

EDDIE. You haven't changed at all.

CAROLINE. You don't think so?

EDDIE. Not a bit. Caroline. I'm so glad to see you.

CAROLINE. I'm glad to see you. Somehow I thought you'd be

sunburned. Living in Dallas.

EDDIE. Remember that time we had a picnic on the beach?

CAROLINE. It was much too early so everyone was shivering, but no one would admit it.

EDDIE. And we ran up and down the beach to get warm.

CAROLINE. And you went swimming!

EDDIE. God, how sorry I was when I got out there in the ocean, but I didn't dare admit it.

CAROLINE. You never would admit when you made a mistake, ever.

EDDIE. I miss you. I still have the letters you wrote me when I was in Europe. I read them sometimes, when I'm alone in my office with nothing to do. And I could kick myself for being so cruel to you, for being such a stupid fool.

CAROLINE. Eddie?

EDDIE. I miss you terribly. I dream sometimes in the middle of the night that I'm falling off a cliff, and I wake up suddenly with a jolt — did you ever do that?

CAROLINE. Yes!

EDDIE. And then I lie awake in the dark for hours and I have the terrible feeling that I've lost someone, and it's you, and you'll never care for me again, and we'll never be together again.

CAROLINE. I care for you, Eddie.

EDDIE. I love you, Caroline.

CAROLINE. Do you?

EDDIE. Always. (*Romantic music swells, and they dance, the wedding dance they never had. The music stops and they stand looking at each other, completely lovestruck.*) I love you, Caroline. I love you. Let's run away.

CAROLINE. Where?

EDDIE. Back to two years ago. Do you think we can do that? Make everything else disappear?

CAROLINE. Yes.

EDDIE. You're just exactly the same.

CAROLINE. Yes! Yes, I am. Exactly the same.

EDDIE. (*Sighing.*) I guess I have to feed you. I invited you to lunch. Where should we go?

CAROLINE. Eddie.

EDDIE. Yes, my love.

CAROLINE. I don't want lunch. (*They kiss.*)

## Scene 13

*The typing pool, one month later. The end of April's bridal shower, with the same decorations from Mary Agnes's shower.*

CAROLINE. Oh, I forgot your present! *(She hands April a wrapped gift. The girls laugh.)*

APRIL. Greenwich Village?

CAROLINE. It wouldn't be your wedding shower without it.

APRIL. I'm going to miss you so much!

CAROLINE. I'll see you in only two months, at your wedding.

APRIL. I'll come back soon for *your* bridal shower!

CAROLINE. You had better! After all of the years of showers for everyone else, there's no one left to put these decorations up for me.

APRIL. It's so strange to be the one after all of this time. *(She looks at her watch.)* I should go. Ronnie is picking me up at the apartment. *(She looks around, emotional.)* Caroline. I'm leaving New York.

CAROLINE. I know.

APRIL. Last night I had everything all packed up in my apartment. The place had never been so neat. And I looked around, and I thought about all of the things that had happened there. And then I thought, "This apartment is awful!"

CAROLINE. Remember how thrilled you were with it when you first moved in?

APRIL. And after I go away, another girl will move in and she'll think it's so wonderful, the way I did. I wish I could leave her a note. Something that says, I know just how you feel.

CAROLINE. No one ever thinks that other people have exactly the same problems and thoughts that she has. You always think you're all alone.

APRIL. *(Looking at Caroline.)* I never felt like that. *(April kisses Caroline on the cheek.)*

CAROLINE. Goodbye, April. Have a safe trip. And happy … happy everything.

47

APRIL. You too. You're going to get what you want too.
CAROLINE. Yes. I think I finally will.


# Scene 14


*Lights up. A few weeks later, the end of the day. Caroline is walking down the hall, daydreaming. Mike Rice enters.*


MIKE RICE. Hey. I've been watching you lately. You look like you're in love.
CAROLINE. I am.
MIKE RICE. I'm glad, Caroline.
CAROLINE. Looks like I'm just a conventional girl after all.
MIKE RICE. The really lucky people find a way to be conventional with an unusual person.
CAROLINE. Well put, Mr. Rice. *(They walk into her office. Eddie is there and he rushes to her.)*
EDDIE. Darling! I wanted to surprise you.
CAROLINE. Eddie! *(She pulls away.)* This is my — this is Mike Rice. He's the editor of *The Cross*. The religious magazine. Mike this is Eddie Harris.
MIKE RICE. Eddie Harris? From Dallas? *(He looks at Caroline, who's embarrassed. Mike holds out his hand to shake.)* I see. Pleased to meet you.
EDDIE. Yes. *(The two men size each other up for a moment.)*
MIKE RICE. I was just on my way out. Miss Bender, I hope you're not going to force Mr. Harris to watch you read manuscripts all evening.
EDDIE. I think I'll be able to entice her away.
MIKE RICE. Undoubtedly. Have a swell evening, kids. *(Mike exits. Eddie goes to the door, closes and locks it.)*
EDDIE. That was close. I should be more careful.
CAROLINE. What does it matter? We're in love.
EDDIE. Helen's father knows a lot of people in publishing. But I've missed you so this past month.
CAROLINE. I've missed *you*! I sit at my desk and do no work at all.

EDDIE. I've been making plans while I've been away.

CAROLINE. Tell me!

EDDIE. Could you be ready to leave New York in a month?

CAROLINE. Leave New York?

EDDIE. I've found you a job in Dallas. It wasn't easy, I was just lucky this turned up. There's a very wealthy, kind of eccentric man who's starting to write a book, and he needs an editorial assistant. You'll be perfect for the job.

CAROLINE. Maybe I should stay here and save up some money. Until we're married.

EDDIE. Darling.

CAROLINE. How long will it take — to get…the divorce?

EDDIE. (Shocked.) Caroline. I can't get a divorce.

CAROLINE. Can't? What do you mean you can't? Why can't you?

EDDIE. It would hurt too many people. It would be the end of my life as it is now, everything, my work, my family, my friends, my home. I can't.

CAROLINE. What about hurting me?

EDDIE. I don't want to hurt you, darling. I couldn't hurt you.

CAROLINE. Don't you think this will hurt me?

EDDIE. I can't marry you. But we can be together forever. Don't you want that?

CAROLINE. How?

EDDIE. You'll take a little apartment, and you'll have this good job, and I'll come visit you. You'll be near me, we'll have lunch together at least twice a week and I'll get away to spend one or maybe even two evenings with you, and we'll speak on the phone every day. Sometimes we'll even be able to manage a whole week-end together.

CAROLINE. Lunch together. One or two evenings when you've escaped from your wife and your respectable married friends? A weekend? What do you want me to be?

EDDIE. I want you to be with me.

CAROLINE. You want me to be your mistress.

EDDIE. Don't say that. It sounds ugly.

CAROLINE. It is ugly.

EDDIE. It won't be ugly for us. We'll make it different.

CAROLINE. (Heartbroken.) So that's your plan to make us both happy. And twenty years from now I'll still be sitting in that little apartment, waiting for you to come and have lunch with me. And

I'll be forty-three years old and I'll never have had any children, or a real home, or someone to love me and care what happens to me.

EDDIE. *(Petulant.)* You make me want to cry.

CAROLINE. I didn't do anything. I only told you what you already knew.

EDDIE. Don't make a decision now. I know it seems sudden. Think it over. I'll call you in the morning.

CAROLINE. Please don't.

EDDIE. *(Beat.)* I was never good enough for you.

CAROLINE. You were.

EDDIE. No. You wanted so much, always pushing me to be interesting and ambitious. You could have married someone else. That's what girls do. They find someone who they like well enough, and they get married. But you're happy living the way you are.

CAROLINE. Happy?

EDDIE. You're the one who's ambitious. And the worst of it is, you're fighting with windmills. If you had talent as an opera singer or a painter or an astrophysicist or something like that, then I'd say it was unavoidable. An artist or a genius can't help it, even a girl. But you're knocking yourself out for this third-rate little publishing company.

CAROLINE. It's hardly little.

EDDIE. Do you honestly think you're doing a job that some other girl couldn't step in and do just as well five minutes after you've left?

CAROLINE. You work for your father-in-law. You have nothing to do. You barely know what your job is!

EDDIE. That's right. I married someone rich and her father gave me a job. And I like it. I like my conventional life.

CAROLINE. Yes. I know. *(Beat.)* Go home to your wife.

EDDIE. I'm just too romantic, that's my trouble. But now I know how things stand. Life is simple, Caroline. You just have to make a choice. *(Eddie leaves. Caroline looks at the open door. The phone rings, and Caroline answers.)*

CAROLINE. Caroline Bender. *(Lights up on David Wilder Savage, in another part of the stage.)*

DAVID WILDER SAVAGE. This is David Wilder Savage. I'm —

CAROLINE. *(Cold.)* I know who you are.

DAVID WILDER SAVAGE. Caroline. Something's happened to Gregg.

CAROLINE. To Gregg? *(Lights shift. We're in the hallway outside of David Wilder Savage's apartment. Gregg enters and talks directly to the audience. As she talks it's as if what she is describing is happening in the moment.)*

GREGG. I was sitting at the top of the stairs outside David Wilder Savage's apartment. David was there. In his apartment, with the girl. There's a scrawl on the wall. It says, "I hate Johnny" That's funny. *(She smiles.)* A girl probably wrote that. *(Happily.)* I hate Johnny. Somebody was coming up the stairs. A man, medium height, with a torn coat and a dirty face. "Hey," he said. "Hey! Hey you girlie!" He started coming towards me. "What's the matter?" He asked. "You lost your key?" I tried to push past him, to escape. I slipped into the little space that was left between him and the wall, and my foot missed the step, and I started to fall. So I reached out. I clawed for a railing, a hand, anything. But there was nothing there. Nothing at all. *(Lights come back up on Caroline and David Wilder Savage. Gregg watches them.)*

CAROLINE. Is she hurt? Where is she? I'll come and get her.

DAVID WILDER SAVAGE. Caroline. I'm sorry. Gregg is dead.
*(Gregg lights a cigarette as the lights fade.)*


## Scene 15


*Later that evening. Caroline is still at her desk, a half-empty bottle of Scotch next to her. Mike Rice enters.*


MIKE RICE. I came as soon as you called.

CAROLINE. I don't want to be alone.

MIKE RICE. No, you shouldn't be. I'll take care of you.

CAROLINE. Do you love me, Mike?

MIKE RICE. I always will. *(He takes her hand. Caroline reaches for him and begins to kiss him, and Mike responds. Caroline is taking off his coat, reaching for the buttons on his shirt, and Mike is letting her. Then he pulls away.)*

MIKE RICE. Caroline. That's not an answer.

CAROLINE. Gregg called Mary Agnes and Brenda "The Grapefruits." She said if you were to slice one of them in half she would be partitioned off into nice little predictable segments, each one the same. But in the end she was the same! She wanted to marry a man who didn't love her. Just like me.

MIKE RICE. Eddie?

CAROLINE. I don't know what's to become of me.

MIKE RICE. Tonight, Gregg, this is bad. But it's not forever. Things will change, they'll be good. They'll get worse again.

CAROLINE. You're not making me feel better.

MIKE RICE. Not a specialty of mine. But I'm your friend. I'm here. And I think Gregg would love for you to show the world a thing or two about not being a Grapefruit.

## Scene 16

*A few weeks later. Caroline's office. Miss Farrow is there. She looks like she's been living in California.*

*Caroline enters, holding a cup of coffee.*

CAROLINE. *(Surprised.)* Miss Farrow? Oh, I don't know your married name.

AMANDA. Miss Farrow is fine. *(Caroline crosses quickly behind her desk.)*

CAROLINE. What brings you to New York?

AMANDA. I'm living here again.

CAROLINE. Oh?

AMANDA. My marriage didn't work out.

CAROLINE. I'm sorry to hear that.

AMANDA. Yes, well ... I suppose I got too used to taking care of myself. *(Amanda loses her composure for a moment.)* I thought you might be married by now, Miss Bender.

CAROLINE. I thought so too.

AMANDA. I hear you've been doing a good job with my writers.

CAROLINE. They're my writers now.

AMANDA. You're very young to be an editor.

CAROLINE. *(Wary.)* My authors like working with me. They're all happy, and I know Mr. Shalimar is happy with my work.

AMANDA. Well, I'm back now. You have a great deal of work to do. I think you can spare a few authors.

CAROLINE. You're not going to take my authors.

AMANDA. I gave them to you in the first place. I'm sure they miss having the benefit of my years of experience.

CAROLINE. *(Gathering her courage.)* Miss Farrow. I don't have your years of experience. But I don't choose books based on their titles. I read everything my writers send me and I encourage them to do better. Sales of my books are more successful than yours ever were. Mr. Shalimar knows that.

AMANDA. This is Mr. Bossart's decision.

CAROLINE. The company owes me something too. I don't make a great deal of money — much less than you did. I've been willing to wait and to do my best. But if you take away any of my authors I'm going to leave. And every single one of them will come with me.

AMANDA. I didn't realize this job meant so much to you, Miss Bender.

CAROLINE. Neither did I.

AMANDA. I see. *(Beat.)* Well. I've found writers from the slush pile before. I can certainly start over again. I'm a very good editor, you know.

CAROLINE. I'm sure that's true.

AMANDA. Perhaps we should have a drink together one night.

CAROLINE. Perhaps we should.

AMANDA. Very good. You'll let me know when you're free.

CAROLINE. I will. *(Amanda turns to leave. Caroline stands.)* Amanda?

AMANDA. Yes? *(Caroline walks toward Amanda. She stands center and looks out.)*

CAROLINE. I'm free now.

## End of Play

# PROPERTY LIST

Toy-sized cruise ship
Manuscripts
Typing paper
Steno pads
Typewriters
Telephones
Intercom
Handkerchief
Lady's hat (Miss Farrow)
Envelope for manuscript
Bottle of Scotch
Cigarette
Lighter
Reports
White lace nightgown
Box of Christmas decorations
Fully stocked bar
Wedding album
4 Man in the Grey Flannel Suit cardboard cutouts
List of authors
Bridal shower decorations
Corsage
Champagne and glasses
Pregnancy pad (Brenda)
*America's Woman* magazine
Whisky glasses
Engagement ring
2 wrapped gifts
Cake
Gold heart necklace
Orange juice
Gin
Cowboy hat
Lady's hat (Caroline)
Purse (Mary Agnes)
Envelope of photos
Argoflex camera in tan case
Purse (April)

Small packing box (April)
Coat
Mail
Pill bottle
Lipstick case
Empty cigarette pack
Half-empty bottle of Scotch
Cup of coffee

# SOUND EFFECTS

Ship horn
Phone ring
Melodramatic underscoring
Cocktail party music with bongos
Party music, then rhumba
Elevator ding
Romantic music
Intercom buzz
Romantic wedding music

# NEW PLAYS

★ **MOTHERHOOD OUT LOUD by Leslie Ayvazian, Brooke Berman, David Cale, Jessica Goldberg, Beth Henley, Lameece Issaq, Claire LaZebnik, Lisa Loomer, Michele Lowe, Marco Pennette, Theresa Rebeck, Luanne Rice, Annie Weisman and Cheryl L. West, conceived by Susan R. Rose and Joan Stein.** When entrusting the subject of motherhood to such a dazzling collection of celebrated American writers, what results is a joyous, moving, hilarious, and altogether thrilling theatrical event. "Never fails to strike both the funny bone and the heart." *—BackStage.* "Packed with wisdom, laughter, and plenty of wry surprises." *—TheaterMania.* [1M, 3W] ISBN: 978-0-8222-2589-8

★ **COCK by Mike Bartlett.** When John takes a break from his boyfriend, he accidentally meets the girl of his dreams. Filled with guilt and indecision, he decides there is only one way to straighten this out. "[A] brilliant and blackly hilarious feat of provocation." *—Independent.* "A smart, prickly and rewarding view of sexual and emotional confusion." *—Evening Standard.* [3M, 1W] ISBN: 978-0-8222-2766-3

★ **F. Scott Fitzgerald's THE GREAT GATSBY adapted for the stage by Simon Levy.** Jay Gatsby, a self-made millionaire, passionately pursues the elusive Daisy Buchanan. Nick Carraway, a young newcomer to Long Island, is drawn into their world of obsession, greed and danger. "Levy's combination of narration, dialogue and action delivers most of what is best in the novel." *—Seattle Post-Intelligencer.* "A beautifully crafted interpretation of the 1925 novel which defined the Jazz Age." *—London Free Press.* [5M, 4W] ISBN: 978-0-8222-2727-4

★ **LONELY, I'M NOT by Paul Weitz.** At an age when most people are discovering what they want to do with their lives, Porter has been married and divorced, earned seven figures as a corporate "ninja," and had a nervous breakdown. It's been four years since he's had a job or a date, and he's decided to give life another shot. "Critic's pick!" *—NY Times.* "An enjoyable ride." *—NY Daily News.* [3M, 3W] ISBN: 978-0-8222-2734-2

★ **ASUNCION by Jesse Eisenberg.** Edgar and Vinny are not racist. In fact, Edgar maintains a blog condemning American imperialism, and Vinny is three-quarters into a Ph.D. in Black Studies. When Asuncion becomes their new roommate, the boys have a perfect opportunity to demonstrate how open-minded they truly are. "Mr. Eisenberg writes lively dialogue that strikes plenty of comic sparks." *—NY Times.* "An almost ridiculously enjoyable portrait of slacker trauma among would-be intellectuals." *—Newsday.* [2M, 2W] ISBN: 978-0-8222-2630-7

**DRAMATISTS PLAY SERVICE, INC.**
440 Park Avenue South, New York, NY 10016  212-683-8960  Fax 212-213-1539
postmaster@dramatists.com  www.dramatists.com

# NEW PLAYS

★ **THE PICTURE OF DORIAN GRAY by Roberto Aguirre-Sacasa, based on the novel by Oscar Wilde.** Preternaturally handsome Dorian Gray has his portrait painted by his college classmate Basil Hallwood. When their mutual friend Henry Wotton offers to include it in a show, Dorian makes a fateful wish—that his portrait should grow old instead of him—and strikes an unspeakable bargain with the devil. [5M, 2W] ISBN: 978-0-8222-2590-4

★ **THE LYONS by Nicky Silver.** As Ben Lyons lies dying, it becomes clear that he and his wife have been at war for many years, and his impending demise has brought no relief. When they're joined by their children all efforts at a sentimental goodbye to the dying patriarch are soon abandoned. "Hilariously frank, clear-sighted, compassionate and forgiving." –*NY Times.* "Mordant, dark and rich." –*Associated Press.* [3M, 3W] ISBN: 978-0-8222-2659-8

★ **STANDING ON CEREMONY by Mo Gaffney, Jordan Harrison, Moisés Kaufman, Neil LaBute, Wendy MacLeod, José Rivera, Paul Rudnick, and Doug Wright, conceived by Brian Shnipper.** Witty, warm and occasionally wacky, these plays are vows to the blessings of equality, the universal challenges of relationships and the often hilarious power of love. "CEREMONY puts a human face on a hot-button issue and delivers laughter and tears rather than propaganda." –*BackStage.* [3M, 3W] ISBN: 978-0-8222-2654-3

★ **ONE ARM by Moisés Kaufman, based on the short story and screenplay by Tennessee Williams.** Ollie joins the Navy and becomes the lightweight boxing champion of the Pacific Fleet. Soon after, he loses his arm in a car accident, and he turns to hustling to survive. "[A] fast, fierce, brutally beautiful stage adaptation." –*NY Magazine.* "A fascinatingly lurid, provocative and fatalistic piece of theater." –*Variety.* [7M, 1W] ISBN: 978-0-8222-2564-5

★ **AN ILIAD by Lisa Peterson and Denis O'Hare.** A modern-day retelling of Homer's classic. Poetry and humor, the ancient tale of the Trojan War and the modern world collide in this captivating theatrical experience. "Shocking, glorious, primal and deeply satisfying." –*Time Out NY.* "Explosive, altogether breathtaking." –*Chicago Sun-Times.* [1M] ISBN: 978-0-8222-2687-1

★ **THE COLUMNIST by David Auburn.** At the height of the Cold War, Joe Alsop is the nation's most influential journalist, beloved, feared and courted by the Washington world. But as the '60s dawn and America undergoes dizzying change, the intense political dramas Joe is embroiled in become deeply personal as well. "Intensely satisfying." –*Bloomberg News.* [5M, 2W] ISBN: 978-0-8222-2699-4

**DRAMATISTS PLAY SERVICE, INC.**
440 Park Avenue South, New York, NY 10016  212-683-8960  Fax 212-213-1539
postmaster@dramatists.com  www.dramatists.com

# NEW PLAYS

★ **BENGAL TIGER AT THE BAGHDAD ZOO by Rajiv Joseph.** The lives of two American Marines and an Iraqi translator are forever changed by an encounter with a quick-witted tiger who haunts the streets of war-torn Baghdad. "[A] boldly imagined, harrowing and surprisingly funny drama." *–NY Times.* "Tragic yet darkly comic and highly imaginative." *–CurtainUp.* [5M, 2W] ISBN: 978-0-8222-2565-2

★ **THE PITMEN PAINTERS by Lee Hall, inspired by a book by William Feaver.** Based on the triumphant true story, a group of British miners discover a new way to express themselves and unexpectedly become art-world sensations. "Excitingly ambiguous, in-the-moment theater." *–NY Times.* "Heartfelt, moving and deeply politicized." *–Chicago Tribune.* [5M, 2W] ISBN: 978-0-8222-2507-2

★ **RELATIVELY SPEAKING by Ethan Coen, Elaine May and Woody Allen.** In TALKING CURE, Ethan Coen uncovers the sort of insanity that can only come from family. Elaine May explores the hilarity of passing in GEORGE IS DEAD. In HONEYMOON MOTEL, Woody Allen invites you to the sort of wedding day you won't forget. "Firecracker funny." *–NY Times.* "A rollicking good time." *–New Yorker.* [8M, 7W] ISBN: 978-0-8222-2394-8

★ **SONS OF THE PROPHET by Stephen Karam.** If to live is to suffer, then Joseph Douaihy is more alive than most. With unexplained chronic pain and the fate of his reeling family on his shoulders, Joseph's health, sanity, and insurance premium are on the line. "Explosively funny." *–NY Times.* "At once deep, deft and beautifully made." *–New Yorker.* [5M, 3W] ISBN: 978-0-8222-2597-3 •

★ **THE MOUNTAINTOP by Katori Hall.** A gripping reimagination of events the night before the assassination of the civil rights leader Dr. Martin Luther King, Jr. "An ominous electricity crackles through the opening moments." *–NY Times.* "[A] thrilling, wild, provocative flight of magical realism." *–Associated Press.* "Crackles with theatricality and a humanity more moving than sainthood." *–NY Newsday.* [1M, 1W] ISBN: 978-0-8222-2603-1

★ **ALL NEW PEOPLE by Zach Braff.** Charlie is 35, heartbroken, and just wants some time away from the rest of the world. Long Beach Island seems to be the perfect escape until his solitude is interrupted by a motley parade of misfits who show up and change his plans. "Consistently and sometimes sensationally funny." *–NY Times.* "A morbidly funny play about the trendy new existential condition of being young, adorable, and miserable." *–Variety.* [2M, 2W] ISBN: 978-0-8222-2562-1

**DRAMATISTS PLAY SERVICE, INC.**
440 Park Avenue South, New York, NY 10016  212-683-8960  Fax 212-213-1539
postmaster@dramatists.com  www.dramatists.com

# NEW PLAYS

★ **CLYBOURNE PARK by Bruce Norris.** WINNER OF THE 2011 PULITZER PRIZE AND 2012 TONY AWARD. Act One takes place in 1959 as community leaders try to stop the sale of a home to a black family. Act Two is set in the same house in the present day as the now predominantly African-American neighborhood battles to hold its ground. "Vital, sharp-witted and ferociously smart." –*NY Times.* "A theatrical treasure…Indisputably, uproariously funny." –*Entertainment Weekly.* [4M, 3W] ISBN: 978-0-8222-2697-0

★ **WATER BY THE SPOONFUL by Quiara Alegría Hudes.** WINNER OF THE 2012 PULITZER PRIZE. A Puerto Rican veteran is surrounded by the North Philadelphia demons he tried to escape in the service. "This is a very funny, warm, and yes uplifting play." –*Hartford Courant.* "The play is a combination poem, prayer and app on how to cope in an age of uncertainty, speed and chaos." –*Variety.* [4M, 3W] ISBN: 978-0-8222-2716-8

★ **RED by John Logan.** WINNER OF THE 2010 TONY AWARD. Mark Rothko has just landed the biggest commission in the history of modern art. But when his young assistant, Ken, gains the confidence to challenge him, Rothko faces the agonizing possibility that his crowning achievement could also become his undoing. "Intense and exciting." –*NY Times.* "Smart, eloquent entertainment." –*New Yorker.* [2M] ISBN: 978-0-8222-2483-9

★ **VENUS IN FUR by David Ives.** Thomas, a beleaguered playwright/director, is desperate to find an actress to play Vanda, the female lead in his adaptation of the classic sadomasochistic tale *Venus in Fur.* "Ninety minutes of good, kinky fun." –*NY Times.* "A fast-paced journey into one man's entrapment by a clever, vengeful female." –*Associated Press.* [1M, 1W] ISBN: 978-0-8222-2603-1

★ **OTHER DESERT CITIES by Jon Robin Baitz.** Brooke returns home to Palm Springs after a six-year absence and announces that she is about to publish a memoir dredging up a pivotal and tragic event in the family's history—a wound they don't want reopened. "Leaves you feeling both moved and gratifyingly sated." –*NY Times.* "A genuine pleasure." –*NY Post.* [2M, 3W] ISBN: 978-0-8222-2605-5

★ **TRIBES by Nina Raine.** Billy was born deaf into a hearing family and adapts brilliantly to his family's unconventional ways, but it's not until he meets Sylvia, a young woman on the brink of deafness, that he finally understands what it means to be understood. "A smart, lively play." –*NY Times.* "[A] bright and boldly provocative drama." –*Associated Press.* [3M, 2W] ISBN: 978-0-8222-2751-9

**DRAMATISTS PLAY SERVICE, INC.**
440 Park Avenue South, New York, NY 10016  212-683-8960  Fax 212-213-1539
postmaster@dramatists.com  www.dramatists.com